ZORN PALMER

# SELF-DISCIPLINE

**The Ultimate Guide to Practicing Self-Discipline, Learn How to Develop Consistent Self-Discipline and Discover How It Can Help You Reach Your Dreams and Achieve Success**

Descrierea CIP a Bibliotecii Naționale a României
ZORN PALMER
    SELF-DISCIPLINE. The Ultimate Guide to Practicing Self-Discipline, Learn How to Develop Consistent Self-Discipline and Discover How It Can Help You Reach Your Dreams and Achieve Success / Zorn Palmer. – Bucharest: Editura My Ebook, 2020
    ISBN 978-606-983-582-1

# ZORN PALMER

# SELF-DISCIPLINE

**The Ultimate Guide to Practicing Self-Discipline,
Learn How to Develop Consistent Self-Discipline
and Discover How It Can Help You Reach Your
Dreams and Achieve Success**

My Ebook Publishing House
Bucharest, 2020

# CONTENTS

# Introduction

My friend Kevin is one of the smartest people I know, hands down. Nobody even comes close.

I went to a pretty good, highly ranked university in California. In my close circle of friends, Kevin outshone everybody else. It's as if he can figure out complicated math equations at the back of his head.

In fact, one time, we were talking about the Heisenberg Uncertainty Principle while eating pizza. There I was, completely stumped about this theory, and my friend Kevin broke it down in between bites of a slice pizza. That's how brilliant he was and still is.

Kevin was so sharp that he only needed to show up in class once, and that is to take roll so that the professor doesn't drop him on the first day, and he'd refuse to go to the class ever again. When exam time rolls around, you can count on Kevin to get at least an A. He did this like clockwork.

In fact, in many cases, he got awards and honors and he didn't even have to show up for the lectures.

I remember laughing when he asked me for any notes that I had for a class he completely ditched. I was laughing because I thought that he was just wasting his time. How can this guy ever pass, much less get an A, when he didn't even bother to show up?

Boy, was I surprised when the guy got better grades than I did. And he didn't cheat. That's how talented Kevin was and still is.

But Kevin, just like most people, has a weakness. We all have our own peculiar and particular shortcoming. It comes with the territory. Kevin is no exception.

His problem was self-discipline. He had a Ferrari engine, but he did not want to drive it in a disciplined, methodical and systematic way.

Now, he is twice divorced, living in an apartment whose rent he could barely afford, and constantly drinking his problems away.

When I think about the life of my friend Kevin, I not only focus on the missed opportunities for career advancement and accomplishments that he is otherwise capable of achieving, I also think about the rest of us. I think about how we missed out because he did not get his act together to fully unlock his potential so the rest of society could benefit from his genius.

Kevin could have been the next dotcom billionaire. He could have been the next Web 2.0 genius that revolutionized technology. But there he is, in the San Francisco Bay Area, struggling to get by on what essentially is a minimum wage.

What's going on? How can somebody with so much potential end up with so little?

It turns out that self-discipline is not a neat little trait that we can choose to have. It is THE trait for ultimate success. Without self-discipline, everything else falls apart.

You may not be the sharpest tool in the shed, and that's okay. As long as you are self-disciplined enough to figure out what you need to learn so you can achieve a little bit more tomorrow, eventually, you'll get there.

Self-discipline is crucial because there are so many distractions trying to divert our attention from what's important and what is truly worthy.

You have to understand that life is full of rewards. But the problem is, the biggest rewards that life has to offer are only attained through a long, sustained period of focused effort.

Discipline is crucial for everything in our lives.

This book gives you a practical framework on how to practice and develop self-discipline so you can become more successful in all areas of your life. It helps you develop a new mindset so you no longer have to continue to struggle.

Eventually, you will reach a point that things seem to magically fall into place. It's not because there is actual magic involved, but because you are so disciplined that opportunities come to you and things start to flow.

You can achieve this state, but the price is high and the journey is long. Are you willing to take that journey?

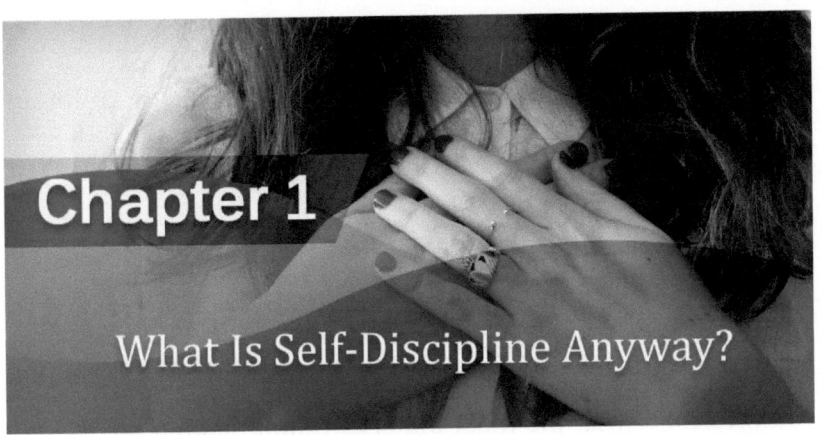

# Chapter 1

## What Is Self-Discipline Anyway?

There are many definitions of self-discipline, but I prefer one supplied by the American philosopher and writer Elbert Hubbard. He said self-discipline is "the ability to do what you have to do when you have to do it, whether you feel like it or not."

Self-discipline is a crucial life skill that enables you to succeed in anything you choose to do. Again, this doesn't necessarily have to do with money. These can involve your relationships. This can also involve your health.

As you probably already know, if you're like most Americans, losing weight is no joke. It requires a tremendous amount of self-discipline because hey, let's face it, when given a choice, we'd rather eat pizza. We'd rather chomp down on a burger or enjoy some fried chicken. But it takes a lot of discipline to eat salad day after day.

### Self-Discipline Enables you to Focus

When you are self-disciplined, you learn how to keep your focus trained on your priorities. You decide on your goals and you prioritize what the most important thing is on a day to day basis.

Once you're able to do that, your self-discipline then kicks in and you're able to zero in on that day after day. Your thoughts, your words, and your actions flow towards that goal.

Of course, you're doing many other things, but there is a recurring theme in your life. There's this consistent focus. You're not just spinning your wheels or chasing your tail.

There is a point to your day because, at the back of your mind, you're inching one step closer to that grand accomplishment. This requires training. It also requires the ability to say no to shallow temptations and shortcuts.

There are plenty of those. In fact, there are too many. When you instead choose to focus on the big picture and take care of the things that you need to focus on, every action you take and every day you spend brings you closer and closer to the desired outcome.

Now, this doesn't mean that your journey is going to be faster. This definitely doesn't mean that your journey will be smooth or everything would be easy.

In fact, when you're working towards a big goal, there are almost always challenges you didn't anticipate. It's as if life is throwing you one curve ball after another.

But, interestingly enough, when you are disciplined, you find it in you to solve those problems and overcome those setbacks as they appear. They don't knock you out. They don't make you quit. They don't rob you of your resolve.

They don't do any of that. Instead, you find it in you to put one foot in front of the other as you move towards that ultimate victory. That is self-discipline.

It's not sexy, and it's not overly dramatic. This is not the movies. It's not like you have all this conspiracy of people working against you and there are all sorts of thrills, chills and spills along the way. No.

In most cases, a personal journey of self-discipline involves doing the same thing over and over again, every day. It's drudgery. There's nothing sexy about it at all.

But your character is changing with each step. You become stronger and stronger as you turn down one temptation after another.

Eventually, you will reach a point where you're saying, "Why am I doing this? There are so many other easier things I can do. There are always that other shortcuts that I could have taken. Why am I doing this?"

You have to find the "why." In other words, you have to find the purpose. Otherwise, it's going to be hard to take that next step.

## Self-Discipline isn't as Hard as You Think

Self-discipline actually isn't as difficult as most people assume. Now, I'm not saying that it's easy. What's important is to understand that it has two phases.

In the first phase, you don't know what you're doing. The task that you're trying to be disciplined at is new to you. It's very challenging at this phase. You're trying to figure things out.

But once you get used to it, there is a tipping point where it becomes easier and easier. You do achieve a point of momentum. The key is to get there.

Once you have fully adjusted, self-discipline actually becomes so easy. Why? It has become a habit. It's almost automatic.

By that point, it didn't really matter what my feelings were. It didn't really matter how inconvenient it was. It had become part of me. This is the power of self-discipline.

Self-discipline is easier than you think once you pass that point of momentum. Self-Discipline is a Choice

There's a common misconception that some people are just born with self-discipline, and most others are not. That's wrong. Self-discipline is a choice.

Do you think a lot of the self-disciplined people out there who achieve victory after victory were born that way? Absolutely not. Often times, it took them crushing defeat to wake up from their old mindsets and choose a more disciplined approach to their life.

The good news is, if they can do it, you can do it too. Self-Discipline Awakens Your Emotional Nature

A lot of people are under the impression that there's really no space for emotion, insight and intuition in self-discipline. They view it as some sort of automatic, almost mechanistic process.

They think that it's soulless. They think that all you need is iron will.

Boy, are these people wrong. If you think about it, self-discipline is really the intuition of understanding, interpreting, and managing your own emotions.

There's a reason why you would rather take things easy. This is your emotional side. It's always tugging at you. It's trying to hold you back and drag you down.

There is a lot of space for emotion here because you're managing your emotional states. And the first part to this is simply becoming aware.

How do I emotionally frame the tasks in front of me? Do I overdramatize things so as to exaggerate their difficulty? Do I make things all that much harder on myself because I view things in such an emotional way?

This is not brute force or unthinking processes. You actually have to get in touch with your emotions and untangle some of the negative feedback loops that you have created for yourself.

## Self-Discipline is One of the Most Pleasurable Things You can Ever Do

I know this is probably going to make you rub your eyes in disbelief. But the truth is, there is a lot of pleasure in self-discipline.

We often associate it with some sort of punishment. After all, we're restricting our lifestyle. We're doing one thing instead of the most pleasurable things that just pop up. We feel that we don't have any freedom.

But the truth is, self-discipline enables you to enjoy the best things in life in their proper timing and context.

With self-discipline, you would know how to provide for yourself and achieve the kind of life you want for yourself and your loved ones. This creates a platform for enjoying the rest of your life.

Let's put it this way, somebody who is disciplined in their career, who reached the highest ranks of their chosen corporate ladder, probably end up with a larger nest egg than everybody else. This enables them to travel the world, take art classes, publish a book or two, and otherwise live life to the fullest. How come? They paid their dues.

So instead of looking at self-discipline as a punishment in and of itself, look at it for what it is: a gateway to greater pleasures.

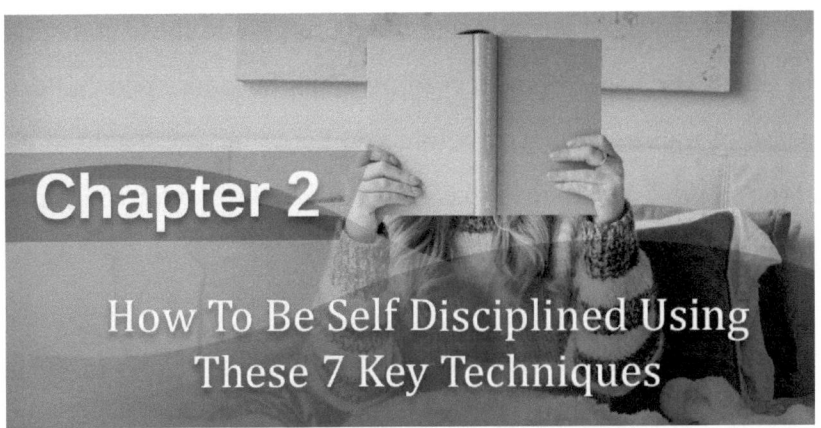

# Chapter 2

## How To Be Self Disciplined Using These 7 Key Techniques

In this chapter, I'm going to give you a quick overview of the 7 techniques that you are going to learn from this book that would enable you to become more self-disciplined. These techniques are laid out in chronological order.

If you're looking for a groundbreaking technique, you're going to be sorely disappointed. These are so basic that you would think that they are common sense – and that is why they're so powerful. They are common and everyday techniques.

The problem is, people don't put them together, much less commit to them. They think that this is so easy that don't even bother to try.

The truth is, there's a lot more difficulty with these techniques than you care to see.

But the good news is that the more you do these and stick to them, the easier the succeeding steps become. You build a sense of momentum. And before you know it, you're able to go through the 7 techniques like clockwork. It eventually becomes part of your daily routine.

### Technique #1: Identify your goals

If you don't know what you're shooting for, don't be surprised if you end up shooting yourself in the foot.

### Technique #2: Prepare a backup plan when temptation arises

Don't get caught flat footed. A little bit of advance preparation goes a long way in helping you overcome temptation each and every time.

### Technique #3: Find your motivation daily

It's very easy for people to dismiss this. People are under the impression that, "Am I not already trying to be self-disciplined? Isn't that motivation enough?"

Well, no. That's not enough because eventually, you start looking at it as a chore. You start looking at your whole personal journey towards discipline as some sort of punishment. What do you do then?

You need to find a way to motivate yourself in a sustainable way so you keep pushing forward. Technique #4: Turn self-discipline into a habit

Eventually, you will reach a point where self-discipline becomes part of your daily routine. The key is to get there. This is the biggest challenge.

Because once you are in the right spot, it's easy to develop a new habit. A lot of your mental reservations have given way, and it has become easier for self-discipline to become part of your daily routine.

## Technique #5: Get enough sleep

Did you know that sleep is crucial to recharging your willpower?

You have to get a full 8 hours of sleep. And it has to be quality sleep for you to fully replenish your willpower on a day to day basis.

## Technique #6: Fill your mind with positive thoughts

It turns out that your thoughts directly impact your reality. How positive you are about your efforts at achieving a certain outcome play a big role in whether those outcomes will materialize at all.

## Technique #7: Surround yourself with self-disciplined people

As I have mentioned previously, it's hard to soar like an eagle when you surround yourself with turkeys. Birds of a feather, after all, do flock together.

# Chapter 3

## Be Clear About Your Goals

If you want to achieve self-discipline, you must have a clear vision of what you want to accomplish. This is non-negotiable. Everything else is a non-starter.

You may have everything figured out, you may even have a solid game plan on how to go about doing things, but none of that matters if you don't have a clear vision of what you seek to accomplish.

## Goals are Not Wishes

I can't even begin to tell you how many people think that they already have goals and plans in life. Well, if you ask them for specific details, it turns out that they don't have goals. They have a clear idea of where they'd like to end up.

There's no shortage of people imagining themselves living in palatial homes, possessing big bank accounts, and driving a fine Italian sportscar. But these are not goals. These are fantasies and wishful thinking.

You know you have a goal when you can take that endpoint of you living in this castle, and then explaining clearly to yourself the backward steps you need to take to get there. That's when you know you have goals.

A clear plan outlines each step you must take in order to reach your goals.

The goals often line up to make larger goals, which produces other outcomes. And these then line up to produce even bigger goals.

For example, if you want to be a lawyer in California, generally speaking, you have to take the bar exam. For that to happen, generally speaking, you have to go to an accredited law school.

Well, the problem is, not just anybody can go to law school. Most of the time, you have to have a college degree or some sort of academic credential. While it does happen that people who did not finish high school can become lawyers, they take a different route.

If you want to take the general route of becoming a lawyer, then that means you have to get a 4-year degree. To get a 4-year degree, you have to apply to college. To apply to college, you have to take an entrance exam.

Do you see how this works? There is the grand goal that you have for yourself, which is to become an attorney, but there are the sub-goals that you have to go through.

You have to go on a journey. And with each victory lies another path that requires another victory. That's how life is, regardless of what endpoint you're looking at.

Your endpoint might be to find yourself in a grand mansion. Great. Awesome. But you have to pay attention to the series of goals that need to be achieved prior to you reaching that endpoint.

**Goals Require Prioritization**

Once you have a clear idea of the steps that you need to take to achieve your ultimate goal, the next step is to set your priorities straight.

You may have a nicely laid out path to go from where you are to where you need to go. That is great. The problem is, if you have other responsibilities, duties and obligations, it's very easy to get lost in the weeds.

It's very easy to think that your job, which doesn't really lead to your goals, is your number one priority. So, you don't take classes. You drop semester after semester because you're working on your job.

The problem here is that your job isn't tied directly to your goal. Sure, your job produces money so you can afford to work on your ultimate goal, but that is the extent of its proper relationship to your goal. Do you see my point?

If you prioritize your job first, then your goal decreases in importance. And before you know it, it goes out of mind. It ceases to be important and you remain stuck where you are.

The moment you decide on your ultimate vision for your life is the moment you must also decide to reprioritize your life.

As important as your job is in putting food on the table, please understand that it's of secondary importance to the grand vision that you are pursuing. Live your life accordingly.

In none of this advice do I say that you drop your job. I'm not saying that at all. That's not what I'm encouraging you to do. Instead, put everything in proper focus and invest your energy accordingly.

### The Great Thing About Crushing Goals

The most awesome thing about crushing goals is that once you clear one hurdle, you get a nice surge of energy and possibility.

For example, when somebody wants to become an attorney, they must first get into college. When they take the SAT and they do well and they get into a good college, it feels good. They built discipline there.

When you free up your energy clearing that first hurdle of getting into a 4-year university, you have to redirect that to the next step, which is to take the LSAT, and finish college with high enough marks to get into a good school.

Once you're there, you need to do well in your first year so you can get a good job with a big law firm or a prestigious practitioner that will open doors for your career later on.

Everything is tied together. And that's why you have to be very careful of how you channel your energy as you clear one hurdle after another.

A lot of people confuse clearing one important goal as an excuse to relax. No. Don't do it that way. That's a nonstarter.

To a certain extent, trying to achieve success by being self-disciplined is like being a shark. Did you know that if a shark isn't swimming, it's dying?

The same goes with you. If you're not pushing forward to the next goal, you're stagnating. And before you know it, you're going to find yourself in a very tough spot.

### Step by Step Guide to Proper Goal Identification

Step #1: Start your day with a list of tasks that you need to accomplish

Knock out one task at a time. Don't get emotionally caught up in each task. Allow the energy and sense of relief released by completing one task to carry over to the next task.

### Step #2: Visualize your grand goal

Think of what you truly desire in your life. I'm talking about your big goals here.

Think about what it would feel like. Think about what you would look like when you are living that kind of life. Come back to this vision before you begin a daily task, and after you complete it.

When you do this, you line up all the small nitty gritty things that you're doing now to something bigger. This reminds your subconscious, as well as your conscious mind, that everything that you do now has meaning. Every step that you take now, ultimately, will lead to the grand victory you are working so hard for.

**Step #3: Write down your grand vision for yourself every day**

In the morning, write down your grand vision. Read it, visualize it, and then crumple the paper. And then, starting with a fresh page of paper, write it down again.

When you do this, you refresh your subconscious and your conscious mind. You also filter out visions and goals that are not really all that important. Maybe you think that you're supposed to go after them because other people desire them.

But if you refresh your life's grand vision this way, a lot of that extra stuff falls out. What's left are the things that are truly important in your life. These are the goals that stick. These are the things that you know, deep down inside, will always remain important to you.

**Step #4: Consciously recommit yourself to your grand goal**

At the risk of sounding corny, you have to look at the list of grand goals and visions for yourself and say to yourself, "I am capable. I have chosen this for myself. I am going to do this."

I'm just giving you those phrases as starting points. Feel free to come up with your own version. What's important here is that you consciously commit to these.

Please understand that it takes years to achieve these. It definitely takes quite a bit of sacrifice.

But the good news is, by being as conscious of these as possible, you burn them into your mind. It becomes part of your daily ritual when you write and rewrite and crumple up the goal list. Eventually, it becomes part of you.

**Step #5: Take action on your goals**

When you're crushing your daily list of tasks, always remember how they relate to your goals. At the end of the day, give yourself some affirmations regarding what you achieved and how they helped you get one step closer to your goal.

This enables you to overcome procrastination. This also pushes you to do your very best in achieving your goals.

This step also makes sure that your goals are at the top of your mind. They are not some distant fantasy or notion that would be nice if it happened. Instead, it becomes immediate.

# Chapter 4

## Always Be Ready With A Backup Plan

Y ou may be thinking that once you've decided to practice self-discipline, it would be smooth sailing. I know that this seems kind of simplistic or even dumb, but let's be honest here. When we make plans, we often think this way.

It may not be obvious to us, but when we look at how we respond to unforeseen circumstances or curve balls that life throws our way, this is our response. It's as if we got blindsided. It never occurred to us that challenges will come.

Make no mistake, when you're trying to practice self-discipline, you're doing something that is not in your nature. Your nature is to take the easy way out, to run towards pleasure, and run away from pain. That is human nature. That's the way we're wired.

You're trying to do something different. You're trying to delay gratification and undergo discomfort now so you can get a massive reward in the future.

Not surprisingly, when people are hit with situations that they didn't anticipate, they are more likely to quit. It hits them from left field. It's such a surprise that it robs them of their resolve.

The better approach is to use the Gollwitzer technique.

In studies conducted in 1997 by the psychologist Peter Gollwitzer, he had study participants give themselves certain "if-then" statements that would enable them to survive all sorts of unintended, unforeseen, and unplanned circumstances. This is called the implementation intention.

Basically, people would work towards a certain goal, but they would give themselves if-then statements if they cannot achieve that goal for some reason.

By having an advanced plan in place, they are not caught by surprise and their willpower is preserved. According to Peter Gollwitzer, this is actually the key to success.

When you pursue your plans and you get hit by surprises, your willpower takes a hit. You don't know what to do, you're confused, and you spend a lot of time diluting your willpower among a wide range of options.

By the time the right option becomes clear, you don't have much willpower left. This reduces your resolve. You feel stuck, discouraged, or, oftentimes, defeated.

By having "if-then" statements planned ahead of time, you're ready to respond regardless of how things turn out. Whether you're waiting or whether you encounter strong opposition, you have a ready plan.

Instead of losing steam and just freezing, you find a way around the problem. And before you know it, you still end up at your intended destination.

This approach was tested in a study that appeared in the journal *Psychology and Health* in March 2009. Study participants were tested ahead of time regarding their intention, behavior and planning regarding consuming more fruits.

It turns out that participants who framed their plans in terms of if-then statements are more likely to eat more fruit than those who just have a more generalized plan of increasing their fruit consumption.

The reason for this is that when all sorts of problems appeared, the people who have if-then plans are able to adjust better and stick with their goal.

## Step by Step Guide to Using Backup Plans Step #1: Create implementation intentions

First, you need to identify the actions that you're going to take to achieve your goal. Also, identify when you need to take those actions.

Once you're clear as to these pairings, come up with possible problems that may appear. Create if- then statements pairing what setbacks may possibly happen and how you plan to deal with them.

## Step #2: Identify how you will deal with problems and lead them to your goal

In other words, don't just focus on getting around a problem that you did not anticipate. Make sure that the action that you plan to take does produce the outcome that you're looking for. In other words, everything must still lead to the goal – even the detours.

For example, instead of saying, "I'm going to lose weight," say, "If it is 6:00 am, I'm going to take a jog."

Now, nowhere in this if-then statement are you saying that you want to lose weight. But when you repeat this over and over again, it becomes obvious. You have a cue, which is a time in the morning, and an action that leads to your goal. When you run or jog in the morning, you are more likely to lose weight.

### Step #3: Be as clear about the obstacles as possible

Come up with a long laundry list of the things that could go wrong. Next, prioritize your list in terms of probability.

### Step #4: Reform your if-then statements with the obstacles in mind Make sure the workarounds still lead to your goal.

### Step #5: Be as specific as possible

It's not enough for you to prepare a backup plan when an unforeseen event happens. It's very important to be as specific as possible regarding the action you need to take and how it leads to your goal.

The clearer you are in terms of your backup action, the more powerful and intentional the backup plan becomes. Before you know it, no curve ball or unforeseen situations will throw you off from your plan.

Don't just simply make goals and hope for the best. That doesn't work. Focus instead on if-then statements that help you deal with reality as your plans unfold.

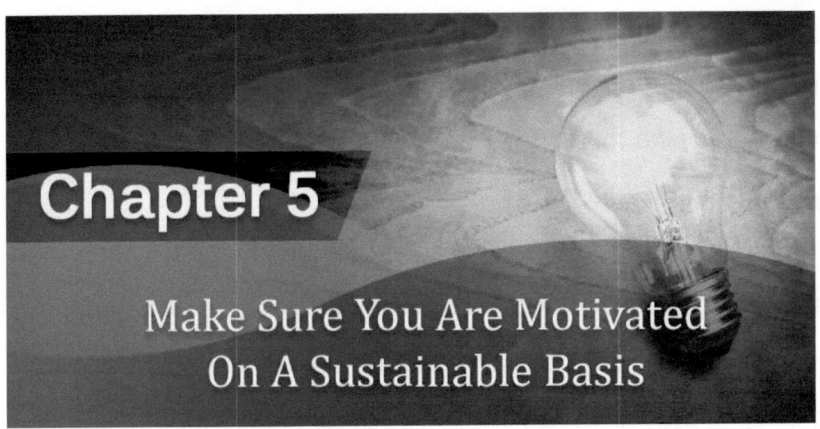

# Chapter 5

## Make Sure You Are Motivated On A Sustainable Basis

L et's get one thing clear. When you decide to become a more self-disciplined person, it's very easy to find the motivation. After all, you just realized how important it is to be self-disciplined. Its benefits are still very clear to you in that point in time.

But as the days go by, you start looking at how difficult it is. You start realizing that it's harder than you originally thought. Sooner or later, your resolve starts to flag. You find yourself slowing down. You start thinking about focusing on other things.

In fact, the temptations start looking better and better. Here you are, working hard at a goal, putting one foot in front of the other, when you could take things easy. Better yet, you can choose to take the day off and just slack off. After all, laziness pays off immediately.

If you find yourself in this situation, I've got some good news for you. Your problem is not your lack of a clear goal. For you to make it this far, your goal has a clear enough purpose to push you. It's worked so far.

It's not lack of advanced planning. By laying out if-then statements that account for things that could go wrong or unforeseen circumstances, you position yourself for ultimate success. Your problem is one of motivation.

Let's put it this way. Even if you were to get a really good looking Ferrari with a very powerful engine, if you don't make a point of keeping enough gas in its gas tank, it will eventually run out of juice. This is not rocket science.

The same applies to practicing self-discipline. You have to have proper motivation every single day. This is the raw material you need that will push you to the point where your self-discipline becomes a habit.

How do you remain motivated? One way, according to a 1999 UCLA study published in the journal Personality and

Social Psychology Bulletin, involves visualization. In other words, you need to visualize the process of you building discipline every single day.

When you zero in on the process, you get motivated about the process. You don't look at it as just something that you do. And, eventually, you start perceiving it as some sort of punishment or ordeal. In this 1999 study, participants were studied in regards to how the envision a certain outcome compared to them getting excited about the process of producing that outcome.

It turns out that when students allow themselves to get motivated by the process of working towards an outcome, they tend to perform better on exams. Compare this with students who were tested and encouraged to get excited about the outcome of the process.

These are 2 totally different things. These 2 groups focus on 2 different areas of the same journey. One group focused on the process. The other group focused on the outcome. Get excited about the process of building discipline. Allow yourself to get pumped up about the fact that you are actually working on building discipline.

A lot of people are not doing what you're doing. You're doing something special. You're putting yourself in a position that would enable you to fine tune a personal trait that will give you a competitive advantage. Get excited about that.

**Step by step guide to creating a self sustaining motivation system Step #1: Think about your life achievements**

Everybody's got some sort of achievement. Examine those achievements. What do they say about you? What kind of strengths can you identify? What kind of personal traits can you build on? Get excited about those.

**Step #2: Figure out what other people see as your strengths and key capabilities**

What do people look up to you for? Who do they see when they look at your life and your life's work? Make no mistake. All of us can be proud of something. Focus on those.

## Step #3: Realize that your achievements were the products of processes

Your achievements were not handed to you. Let's get that clear. You had to work for them. They are part of a process. Whether it's long or short, you still had to put in the work. Identify what those processes are. Realize that you went through those processes just as you are going through a process right now.

## Step #4: Draw an association between the past processes you went through and the one you're going through now

When you realize that the process that you are going through now in your journey to greater success is really not much different from a similar path that you have traveled down before, you should get a tremendous sense of reassurance.

You're not doing something completely new. You've been down this path before. This should give you peace of mind.

You're not going through uncharted territory. The best part? You've done it before.

What's holding you back from doing it now?

Get excited about this process because you've done it before. It's already delivered positive results. Wait until this journey delivers even greater results. This is how you get excited about the process instead of just obsessing about the final outcome.

# Chapter 6

## Turn Self-Discipline Into A Habit

Please understand that really successful people who are very self-disciplined weren't born that way. They made certain choices. One choice is to turn self-discipline into a habit. The good news is self- discipline is just like any other life skill.

At first, it's kind of rough because you haven't really focused on it before. In fact, in many cases, you might be operating in fully foreign territory. It's completely new to you. Its language is Greek to you.

But as you figure things out through trial and error and by sheer repetition, eventually, everything starts to fall into place and guess what happens. It becomes easier. It's not much different from going to the gym the first time.

If you've ever tried working out at the gym, the first few days are murder on your muscles. How can they not? You haven't put pressure on your muscles before. But as you get used to pumping iron and you go to the gym day after day, eventually, your body adjusts.

Before you know it, you start developing leaner, bigger and stronger muscles. The same applies to your self-control and self-discipline. Instead of physical muscles, they are mental and emotional muscles. Still, they operate like muscles.

The more you challenge them and put pressure on them, the stronger they become. There is, of course, initial resistance and discomfort. This goes with the territory. But as long as you are able to follow through, eventually, things become easier and, before you know it, becomes almost automatic because self-discipline has become a habit.

In a 2010 study published in the journal of Experimental Social Psychology, 92 people who were trying to quit smoking were studied in terms of self-control habit formation. In an initial meeting, they were lead to believe for 2 weeks that when they do certain tasks like keeping a diary, doing math problems, practicing hand grip exercises and avoiding sweets, this would build self-control.

In the first group involving hand grip and sweet avoidance, participants were told to inhibit their behaviors, feelings and urges. They were told to eat as little sweet foods as possible.
46

They were also given hand grips to exercise their gripping power.

For the diary group, people were just told to keep a diary of any acts of self-control they did throughout the period. This was actually the control group.

It turns out that when people were assigned to practices involving resisting sweets or doing hand grip exercises, they are more likely to achieve higher levels of self-control. In other words, small acts of self-control can lead to greater overall self-discipline.

It becomes a habit. When you apply self-control to small things, they scale up to the larger challenges in your life. Don't think that a little bit of self-control in one area of your life will, in no way, spill over to other areas of your life. They do.

**Step by step guide to turning self-control into a habit**
**Step #1: Focus on getting small stuff done**

If, for example, you're trying to adopt a new habit of always knocking out your daily to-do lists, focus first on getting small stuff done. Focus on the ministerial stuff.

### Step #2: Scale up once it gets easy

When you look at your daily tasks, there are always low hanging fruit. Make it a point to habitually eliminate those day after day. Once you've reached a point where it becomes easy for you to take care of low hanging fruit, scale up to tasks that take a lot more time or require more willpower.

### Step #3: Keep scaling up when things get easy

You will notice something strange when you're scaling up. It turns out you achieve a certain momentum and you're able to handle more things. Pay close attention when this happens. Compare yourself to when you began.

### Step #4: Get your if-then statements ready

Always have your if-then statements at the back of your mind when it comes to intention implementation. A little bit of preparation can go a long way because life can throw you curve balls. Be prepared for disappointments and circumvent them.

There's always a work around. So focus on the workaround and you'd be surprised as to how much you can achieve. The best part to all of this is your momentum builds up very quickly over time.

# Chapter 7

## Make Sure You Get Enough Sleep

Self-discipline, just in case you're not aware, eats up a lot of your personal focus and willpower. According to researchers, it turns out that we only have a certain amount of willpower available to us every single day.

It's not like we have this unlimited reservoir of willpower that we just need to tap. That doesn't exist. We're not wired that way. Instead, imagine yourself having a certain number of coins every single day. Anything that requires attention, analysis, focus or any kind of critical or deep thinking burns quite a bit of willpower.

The same applies to any kind of activity that requires patience. It is no surprise that a lot of people who have serious self-control issues run out of willpower before the day is out. In fact, a lot of them don't start out with much willpower at all.

Even fairly mid-level challenges are enough to deplete their willpower. So, what happens to them? Well, they're unable to resist temptation for the rest of the day. They basically just go back to their old patterns of trying to seek a shortcut or just basically procrastinating and putting things off.

They don't build self-control and self-discipline. They don't have the foundation for it. How can they? They've completely run out of willpower.

Well, it turns out that this fixed amount of willpower that we start out with can be increased based on how much we sleep the night before. Sleep is crucial to replenishing your willpower.

If you notice that you don't have much willpower to begin with, try getting a full 8 hours worth of sleep. Please pay attention to what I just said. I'm not just talking about the duration of your sleep. It's crucial for you to get 8 full hours of shut eye. That's important.

But you also have to pay attention to quality in addition to quantity. It's not enough to get 8 hours of sleep. It has to be the right kind of sleep. What is the best quality sleep? We're talking about REM sleep. This is rapid eye movement sleep where you're basically dreaming.

Your mind unclutters itself. It reorganizes information and it rests in a deep and profound way. When it does this, your mental faculties are refreshed the next day and you start off with a lot more willpower than the day before. That's how REM sleep works.

You have to burn the candle from both ends when it comes to sleep. Not only do you have to make sure that you sleep long enough, but it also has to be deep, restful, meaningful sleep. When you do this, you increase the amount of willpower you have and your mood is able to withstand a lot more punishment. You are able to focus for much longer, exercise better judgment and improve your choices overall.

These conclusion were inferred from a study published in October 2011 in the academy of management journal. 2 groups were studied in terms of sleep deprivation and the study highlights the fact that those study participants who had less sleep had showed signs of decreased self-control. They also tended to be more hostile.

**Step by step guide to increasing your sleep quality and quantity Step #1: Keep a regular sleep schedule**

Make sure that regardless of whatever else is going on in your life, you stick to a fixed schedule for sleep. You owe yourself 8 hours every single night. Stick to that schedule. If you find yourself waking up in the middle of the night, stay in your bed.

Resist the temptation to get up, grab a glass of water or check your email. The moment you're exposed to light, chances are your sleep patterns will be disrupted and you're going to have a tough time going back to sleep.

If you find yourself waking up in bed, stay in bed.

**Step #2: Make it a point to lay down and get up at the same time every single day**

**At first, it's going to be tough for you to stick to this schedule. But eventually, you will get used to it. Step #3: Adopt a pre and post sleep ritual**

Believe it or not, the things that you choose to do before and after you sleep play a big role in both the duration and quality of your sleep. Be very careful as to what your rituals are.

Don't drink coffee. Don't drink any kind of stimulants. Don't work out or engage in heavy exercise right before you go to sleep.

Manage your time very carefully. Pay close attention to what you choose to do before and after your sleep. Take notes. Maybe there are certain activities that enable you to fall asleep faster and deeper. Do those.

By the same token, be aware of the things that you're currently doing that cuts your sleep short or ensure that your sleep is very shallow. Ditch those and replace those with better habits.

## Step #4: Take control of your surroundings

A lot of people think that just because their bed is at a certain place in their home and it has a certain surrounding that basically, they have nothing they can do about it. This is wrong. You have a lot of say in your surroundings before you sleep.

You might want to remodel your bedroom. You might want to move furniture around. You might want to make small changes in lighting and acoustics as well as background sound. Don't think that just because your bed is located in a certain place that sleep is a take it or leave it proposition. Don't fall into that trap.

Make sure that your surroundings are conducive to sleep. Unfortunately, the only person that can definitively answer this is you. So pay close attention to your surroundings. Take control of them. Make small changes here and there.

Mix and match things. Track your results. Build on that things that you're doing right, identify the things that you're doing wrong and come up with variations. This can take quite a while, but the good news is you will be paid off handsomely in the form of longer and more rewarding sleep.

Your self-control is on the line. You need as much willpower in the beginning of the day as possible. Consider this long, drawn out process as unnecessary investment in the willpower you need to achieve the self-control that you're looking to build.

# Chapter 8

# Think Positively

When was the last time you tried playing basketball? If you're like most Americans, you probably played hoops at least once. Now, imagine yourself dribbling and stepping near the line and then taking a shot. Pretty straightforward, right?

Well, imagine thinking to yourself that the ball is not going to go through the hoop. You're assuming the worst. You're assuming an air ball. You're assuming that you're going to shoot a brick. Whatever it is you're imagining, it's not going to end well.

What do you think happens to your chances of making that shot? Well, it should not be a surprise to anybody that you miss every shot you take. You see, your performance in anything in your life is closely related to how you choose to think about your prospects.

If you have a very pessimistic view of how things will turn out, then don't be all that shocked when everything you think about becomes some sort of self fulfilling prophecy. If you think you're not going to make that shot, your emotions are in a certain place.

You start doubting yourself. Before you know it, this has a tremendous impact on your actual physical performance. Maybe you don't aim the shot properly. Maybe you take the wrong body position.

Whatever the case may be, the ball doesn't go through the hoop.

Now, apply this to all other situation in your life. It fits hand in glove. How you choose to think about situations in your life has a very important role to play in how things turn out. In fact, according to a research from the university of Michigan published in May 2005, ones level of mental positivity correlates with the amount of willpower they have available to them to do important things. This is crucial.

In the Michigan study, students were shown short film clips that either created feelings of joy, contentment or neutral emotion. Other groups were also shown film clips that triggered negative emotions.

After seeing all these images, the participants were given a piece of paper that started out with the phrase "I would like to". It turns out that the students who were shown negative images showed the least amount of plans.

On the other end, people who were shown images of contentment and joy listed out longer plans. In other words, when you experience emotions like love, contentment, inner peace and joy, you're more likely to see the possibilities of your life.

You're more likely to see things as open ended and full of adventure and possibility. In other words, you're more likely to take action. You're also more likely to tap into your willpower to make things happen.

This is crucial to building self-control. When you have a positive mood produced by a positive state of mind, you're more likely to roll with the punches when you are confronted with set backs. Make no mistake, as you seek to build self-discipline, you will be hit by set backs. It comes with a territory.

While a previous technique teaches you to be prepared for such setbacks, by preparing "if-then" statements, you need willpower to turn those statements into reality. You need willpower to overcome challenges.

This is very hard to do when you have a negative mindset. This is almost impossible if you are upset or in, otherwise, a very negative mood.

**Step by step guide to thinking more positively Step #1: Start your day with positive affirmations**

Tell yourself that today will be an awesome day. It's not enough to call it a good day, it's going to be an awesome one. At first, you probably won't believe yourself. It just feels like you're going through the motions.

But when you allow yourself to focus on the statement "This will be an awesome day!", eventually, your mind will start making associations. It will start achieving certain things during the day. The positive association is made.

The next time you repeat your positive affirmation to yourself, it starts sounding more and more like reality. The key is to allow it to work its effects on you. You probably would have to repeat it over and over again until that association is made.

## Step #2: Actively police negative self talk

Have you ever stubbed your toe and called yourself an idiot? Have you ever been embarrassed by people or you made a public mistake? In the back of your head, you're thinking "I'm such a loser." Well, that is negative self talk.

You're just saying that to say it. If left unchecked, that will be your reality. You think you're a loser now? Well, wait until your negative affirmation kicks in and it becomes your hard reality.

You have to nip this in the bud. Think of what you're saying to yourself on a day to day basis. Try to turn things around. For example, if you're constantly saying "I have no chance with her" or "I suck at this," and turn things around.

Ask yourself questions. "What do I need to do today to be 1% better than yesterday?" "How do I treat her today that will make her treat me better by 1% today?" Something along those lines.

When you ask these things to yourself, you're asking for solutions. You're not condemning yourself to a certain reality. You're not saying to yourself, "You're a clown. You're a loser.

Nobody likes you." Instead, you're saying to yourself "How do I tap my almost inexhaustible supply of imagination, resourcefulness and cleverness to create a better reality for myself?"

Ask yourself questions. The more open ended, the better. You'd be surprised as to how quickly your mind fills in the details.

## Step #3: Avoid negative triggers

Make no mistake. The human mind is a very powerful association machine. It creates all sorts of positive associations. It also creates negative associations. If you know what your negative triggers are and that certain places, people, media and other things bring out the negativity in you, it's your job to avoid those things.

That's the bottom line. At first, start with avoidance. Eventually, once you have enough willpower and you have enough discipline, start turning those associations around. Still, you have to begin with avoidance.

## Step #4: Actively look for the best in things

I made this step the last one because it's the most difficult. However, it's also the most rewarding. Once you're able to achieve the steps above, actively look for the victory in everything you do. You will quickly realize that there are actually a lot of positive things happening around you.

You only need to choose to become aware of them. It doesn't have to be big. They don't have to be overly dramatic. They just have to be real. Believe it or not, being able to wake up every single day with both your kidneys functioning is a great thing.

If you don't believe me, wait until you develop kidney stones. They are not pleasant. Being able to breathe naturally is a blessing. If you don't believe me, just go to your nearby cancer ward and ask the local community coordinator to see if you can talk to and soothe people suffering from lung cancer.

I know it may seem like a small comfort because you don't know where your rent money's going to come from. Your girlfriend just left you. Your boss is an idiot and overbearing dictator. But focus on the small things that are going right.

Once you're able to notice that there are many things going right, your focus starts to change. And the more you focus on those, the more they grow. The more you become grateful. And once you're in that right frame of mind, it starts changing your ability to withstand the things that are not so positive in your life.

That's how you get over.

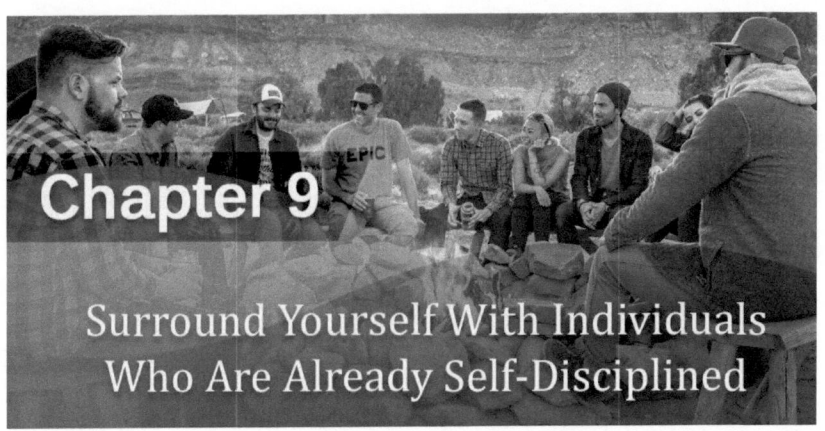

# Chapter 9

## Surround Yourself With Individuals Who Are Already Self-Disciplined

There's a lot of truth to the old saying "birds of a feather flock together." How come? Human beings are sponges. We soak up our surroundings. Part of the reason why you're having a tough time doing what you need to do when you need to do it is because you hang around with people who are always taking a short cut.

Worse yet, you may be hanging around with people who tell you that you can't do it. Your only option, as far as they're concerned, is to do exactly what they're doing. It's very hard to soar like and eagle when you choose to surround yourself with chickens, turkeys and other fowl.

You know what you're capable of. You know how high you can soar because you can dream that far. It really would be quite tragic when you choose to surround yourself with such small minded people that they create some sort of motivation black hole for you.

No matter how bright your dreams are, all their vibrancy and life gets sucked out by the negativity of people around you. All you can hear is "You can't do it! I've tried and failed. Don't be like me."

The worst part to all of this is the fact that often times, these people are our family members. How many times have your parents discouraged you? How many times have your cousins told you that you shouldn't even try. How many times have a well-intentioned uncle or aunt put you under their arms and told you that they sympathize with you, but you just don't have it in you?

You have to understand that these people don't have it in for you. They want you to be happy. They want you to be content. They want good things for you. But the problem is they are so jaded or they have been distorted by past mistakes and failures that they feel that they're doing you a favor by discouraging you.

Deep down inside, they just don't want you to be disappointed as they are. Life let them down and they'd be damned if they would let somebody they love, namely you, go through the same ordeal.

Please understand that in most cases, it's love that animates them. They don't want you to lose your resolve. They don't want you to lose your will. Instead, they just don't want you to get hurt. So in their minds, the shortcut to that is to not try at all.

You need to get out of that motivational black hole. You need to do it pronto. How do you do that? Surround yourself with people who have already achieved some of what you're trying to achieve. If you are at work, chances are 20% of the people there produce 80% of the results.

Your job on day 1 is to find those people. Hang out with them. Sure, at first, they probably would doubt you. They might even be very suspicious. But earn their trust. Get in their inner circle. Tell them "You have what I need. You are the winners in this organization. Sure, I'm wet behind the ears and I'm not tried nor am I proven. But you can trust my sincerity that I am looking to learn from you."

Besides the nice little ego boost, you appeal to the better angels of their nature because they know how hard it was to start out being nobody. They know how tough the process can be. If they can see your sincerity and the clear drive in your eyes to want to improve yourself, they see themselves in you.

In fact, the very best ones would love to pay it forward. In other words, nobody was there for them to show them the ropes. But now that they have a chance to mentor somebody, they will jump at that chance.

That shows you their real nature. So hang out with those people. Real coaches will not sugar coat anything. They will tell you that it's rough. But they will also tell you that there is always a way out and this means learning the lessons that you need to learn and just powering through until you achieve momentum.

But people are not going to waste their time on you until you show them that you're willing to pay the price. This means hanging out with them. This means trying to make the effort to hang out with them. In fact, a lot of them will test you.

They'll say to themselves "Does this kid really want to be a top sales person in this organization? Let me bust his chops. Let me give him a hard time." You just need to get over this. Once you earn their trust and confidence, they will clue you in on the secret.

**Step by step guide to surrounding yourself with self-disciplined mentors Step #1: Find the winners in your organization**

By winners, I'm not talking about the CEO. I'm talking about mid level people. Find them. They can always be found in any organization. Like I said, 20% of the people in any organization produce 80% of that organizations result. Find that 20%.

**Step #2: Prove your worth**

Don't just hang out for social purposes. They know that people like that are leeches. They want the appearance of success, but are unwilling to do any of the work to achieve real success. Real successful people don't have time to for such people. They're parasites.

Since the most productive people in your organization which one you are, don't be all that shocked if they try to test you. Maybe they'll give you an assignment. Maybe they'll try to work with you and test your chops.

**Whatever the case may be, get ready for the test. Be prepared to ace that exam. Step #3: Keep an open mind to critique so you are accountable**

The worst thing that you can do is to have an ego. The worst thing that you can do when you're trying to learn from a mentor is to think that that person doesn't know what they're doing and that you're always right.

I know this sounds crazy. But people do this all the time. They think that they're complete. They think that they've figured everything out. So when somebody who actually has figured things out tries to mentor them, nothing sinks through.

Everything is seen as some sort of offensive remark. People feel that they're being attacked. So they don't learn. You can't take this personally. You're the student. Act like one. You don't see a student go up to a professor and say "You're wrong! You don't know what you're talking about!"

How would you know? You haven't read the book backwards and forwards. You haven't done the research. You haven't been asked to speak in hundreds of symposiums and conferences. You better shut up and sit down because every time you open your mouth, you're not learning.

It's much better to close your mouth and open your ears. The fact that you are shutting down your ego or setting aside pride is a self-discipline exercise in of itself. Hey, let's face it. All of us want to be primadonna. So all of us want the spot light.

But the problem is when you hog the spot light and you try to put on a show, you're not learning. These people have what you're looking for. So allow yourself to learn.

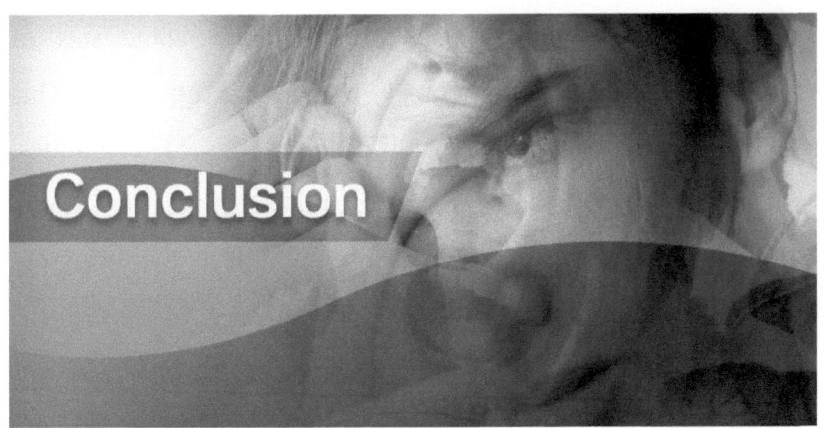

# Conclusion

Self-discipline is a vital life skill. It is crucial to any kind of success. In fact, if you were to pick 3 top traits that will help ensure your success, self-discipline is one of them. Another one is grit or determination.

The truth is, you can get that fantastic life you have dreamed all your life for through self-discipline. You don't necessarily have to be the sharpest tool in the shed. You don't have to be born with a PhD. You don't have to be a rock star coming in through the door.

With enough self-discipline, you will learn what you need to learn to do what you need to do for however long it takes to achieve the big things. The best part about self-discipline is you get a big picture view of the process.

It humbles you. It doesn't turn you to some sort of primadonna who is continuously hungry for attention. This enables you to start looking at life as a series of techniques. Instead of seeing it as a series of humiliations that beat the life out of you, you start seeing life as a series of tests that bring out the best in you.

Far from a scary fire that consumes people and produces excruciating pain, purifying fire refines people just as fire refines gold. When gold is passed through the fire, it becomes pure, it becomes bright and its value shines out.

This is the process of discipline. It's not painless by any stretch of the imagination. But it is necessary pain. I wish you nothing but the greatest success.

9 786069 835821

Printed by Libri Plureos GmbH in Hamburg,
Germany